Creative Mind
and Success

TITLES BY ERNEST HOLMES

Published by Tarcher/Penguin

365 Science of Mind
The Art of Life
Creative Mind
Creative Mind and Success
The Essential Ernest Holmes
The Hidden Power of the Bible
Love and Law: The Unpublished Teachings
Prayer
The Science of Mind: The Definitive Edition
This Thing Called You

JEREMY P. TARCHER/PENGUIN

a member of Penguin Group (USA) Inc.

New York

Creative Mind

and Success

ERNEST HOLMES

JEREMY P. TARCHER/PENGUIN
Published by the Penguin Group
Penguin Group (USA) Inc., 375 Hudson Street, New York, New York 10014, USA · Penguin Group
(Canada), 90 Eglinton Avenue East, Suite 700, Toronto, Ontario M4P 2Y3, Canada (a division of
Pearson Penguin Canada Inc.) · Penguin Books Ltd, 80 Strand, London WC2R 0RL, England ·
Penguin Ireland, 25 St Stephen's Green, Dublin 2, Ireland (a division of Penguin Books Ltd) ·
Penguin Group (Australia), 250 Camberwell Road, Camberwell, Victoria 3124, Australia (a division
of Pearson Australia Group Pty Ltd) · Penguin Books India Pvt Ltd, 11 Community Centre,
Panchsheel Park, New Delhi–110 017, India · Penguin Group (NZ), 67 Apollo Drive, Rosedale,
North Shore 0632, New Zealand (a division of Pearson New Zealand Ltd) · Penguin Books (South
Africa) (Pty) Ltd, 24 Sturdee Avenue, Rosebank, Johannesburg 2196, South Africa

Penguin Books Ltd, Registered Offices: 80 Strand, London WC2R 0RL, England

First trade paperback edition 2004
First Jeremy P. Tarcher/Penguin edition 1997
Copyright © 1919 by Ernest Holmes, 1957 by Church of Religious Science

Published simultaneously in Canada

Most Tarcher/Penguin books are available at special quantity discounts for bulk purchase for sales
promotions, premiums, fund-raising, and educational needs. Special books or book excerpts also can be
created to fit specific needs. For details, write Penguin Group (USA) Inc. Special Markets, 375 Hudson
Street, New York, NY 10014.

The Library of Congress catalogued the hardcover edition as follows:

Holmes, Ernest, 1887–1960.
Creative mind and success / by Ernest Holmes.
p.   cm.
Reprint. Originally published: New York: R. M. McBride, c1919.
1. United Church of Religious Science—Doctrines.   2. Success—Religious aspects.
3. New Thought.   I. Title.
BP605.U53H635   1989   89-3668 CIP
299'.93—dc19
ISBN 0-87477-866-2

ISBN 1-58542-268-1 (paperback edition)
ISBN 978-1-58542-608-9 (paperback reissue)

Printed in the United States of America
1   3   5   7   9   10   8   6   4   2

BOOK DESIGN BY NICOLE LAROCHE

A Word from the Author

This foreword is being written in 1957 for the nineteenth printing of this little book. I have just re-read it—probably for the first time since it originally appeared in 1919.

And as I read, I contemplated what changes might have occurred in my thinking during these thirty-eight years, what revisions I might make in the manuscript if I were writing it today.

They were few—for Truth is ageless, timeless, changeless. We may have modified our techniques slightly, for we certainly should make improvements in nearly four decades of experience with the Law of Mind in Action. For example, we no longer "hold thoughts." We *think* positive thoughts— and then release them, charged with the spiritual energy of Faith, into the Universal Mind which is common to all men.

Neither do we use the "power of *will*" to set the Law in motion. We use our God-given power of *choice*—either to use the Law constructively or destructively.

This much I know—that if I were writing this book today, it would be penned with far greater conviction than in 1919, for during these intervening years I have witnessed *proof* in hundreds of cases that "all is Love, yet all is Law" in the realm of Mind.

At that time I wrote: "Already thousands are using this great Power, and thousands are eagerly watching and waiting for the new day."

It is gratifying to note that during these thirty-eight years, many more thousands have learned the Truth that sets men free—free from the man-made dogmas and superstitions that have fettered man's thinking down through the centuries.

I am more convinced than ever that the Science of Mind, as expounded in our text-book under that name, based upon the teachings of Jesus and co-ordinated with the philosophy of other great thinkers of the ages, is destined to become the new religion for the new day.

It is a self-evident truth that if man is made in the spiritual image and likeness of God, man's mind must be made out of God's Mind; also that man has the same power in his individual life that God has in the Universal. If it is true that, as Jesus said, "it is the Father within, He doeth the works"— then man's inner life is one with the Father.

Since all causation is mental, it follows that if all things are created by the Mind of God and man's mind is part of God's Mind, man is able, by thinking, to set in motion a Power that creates. Of course, man does not create that Power, neither does he coerce it. It is his to use either rightly or wrongly. It is always with him. It never deserts him. It operates every moment of his life.

We need, therefore, only to clear our minds of unbelief, and know that "it is done unto us as we believe." In this spirit, we can think thoughts of success and success will follow as surely as day follows night, for our thought will not return unto us void. "It is the Father's good pleasure to give us the kingdom." We need only accept it.

Even when we fail, we are proving that the Law works— according to our belief that it will *not* work. Of course, we do not wish to fail, but if our mental attitude is one of doubt, then the result will be the out-picturing of our negative thoughts. We can change the effect only by changing the cause . . . by reversing our thoughts and believing that the good we desire is already ours.

Knowing this, we can no longer blame others for our troubles. We recognize that within ourselves is the Power to produce success or failure.

Fear brings failure; faith brings success. It's just that simple.

If you keep that in mind as you read the contents of this little book, you will find it a delightful spiritual adventure.

ERNEST HOLMES

January 1957

Contents

PART ONE
Instruction

PART TWO
Practice

Creative Mind
and Success

AN INQUIRY
INTO THE TRUTH

An inquiry into Truth is an inquiry into the cause of things as the human race sees and experiences them. The starting point of our thought must always begin with our experiences. We all know that life *is*, else we could not even think that we are. Since we *can* think, say and feel, we *must* be. We live, we are conscious of life; therefore we must be and life must be. If we are life and consciousness (self-knowing) then it follows that we must have come from life and consciousness. Let us start, then, with this simple fact: *Life is and life is conscious of itself.*

But what is the nature of this life; is it physical, mental, material or spiritual? A little careful thinking based upon logic, more than any merely personal opinion, will do much in clearing up some of these questions that at first seem to stagger us with their bigness.

How much of that which *is* may we call life? The answer would have to be: Life is *all* that there is; it is the reason for all that we see, hear, feel—all that we experience in any way. Now nothing from nothing leaves nothing, and it is impossible for something to proceed from nothing. Since something is, that from which it came must be all that is. *Life, then, is all that there is.* Everything comes from it, ourselves included.

The next question is, How do things come from life? How do the things that we see come from the things that we do not see? The things that we see must be real because we see them. To say they are not real will never explain them nor answer any question about them. God's world is not a world of illusion but one of divine realities. The truth must not explain away things that we see. It must explain what they are. We are living and experiencing varying degrees of consciousness and conditions. Only when the why of this living and of our experiences is understood will we know the least thing about the truth. Jesus did not say that things are illusions. He said that we must not judge from the standpoint of the seen but must judge righteously or with right judgment; and He meant that we must get behind the appearance and find out what caused it. So let us not in any way fool ourselves nor allow ourselves to believe we have always been fooled. We are living in a world of realities. Whatever we have experienced is a reality insofar as that experience is concerned, although if we had had a higher understanding of life, the unpleasant experience might have been avoided.

WHAT LIFE IS

I n the first place, what do we mean by life? We mean that which we see, feel, hear, touch or taste, and the reason for it. We must have come into contact with all we know of life. We have already found what life is, or we could not have had any of these experiences. "In the beginning was God," or life. Out of this life which is, everything which is is made. So life must flow through all things. There is no such thing as dead matter. Moreover, life is one, and it cannot be changed except into itself. All forms are forms of this unity and must come and go through some inner activity. This inner activity of life or nature must be some form of self-consciousness or self-knowing. In our human understanding we would call this inner knowing, or consciousness, "thought." The Spirit, or Life, or God, must make things out of Himself, through self-recognition, or self-knowing or, as we would call it— *thinking*. Since God is all, there is nothing to hinder Him from doing what He wishes, and the question "How do things come into being?" is answered: God makes them out of Himself. God thinks, or knows, and that thing which He thinks or knows appears from Himself, and is made out of Himself. There is no other possible explanation for what we see. Unless people are willing to begin here, they will never understand how it is that things are not material but spiritual.

MAN'S PLACE IN CREATION

But where does man come in? He *is*. Therefore it follows that he, too, is made out of God, since God, or Spirit, is all. Being made out of God, we must partake of His nature, for we are "made in His image."

Man is a center of God in God. Whatever God is in the Universal, man must be in the individual world. The difference between God and man is one of degree and not of quality. Man is not self-made; he is made out of God.

The question might arise, why did God do this? No living person can answer this question. This is something that is known only of the Father. We might suppose that God made man to live with Him and to enjoy with Him, to be one with the Father. It is true, indeed, that those who have felt this most deeply have had a corresponding spiritual power that leads us to suppose that God really did make man as a companion. Man is the individual and God is the Universal. "For as the Father has life in Himself, so has He given to the Son to have life in himself." Man's mind is made out of God's mind, and all that man is or ever will be, all that he has or ever will have, must partake of the Divine nature. Man did not make it so, but it is so, and he must accept the fact and see what he can do with it. If he has the same power in his individual life that God has in the Universal, then this discovery will mean freedom from all bondage when he learns how to use his power. As God governs His Universal world so will man govern his individual world, always subject to the greater law and life. This could not be otherwise if we realize what follows from it, for so realizing we find ourselves living in a very different world from the one in which we thought we were living. God governs not through physical law as result, but first by inner knowing—then the physical follows. In the same way, man governs his world by the process which we will call, for want of a better name, the power of his thought.

Man's inner life is one with the Father. There can be no separation, for the self-evident reason that there is nothing to separate him from God, because there is nothing but life. The separation of two things implies putting a different element between them; but as there is nothing different from God, the unity of God and man is firmly established forever. "My Father and I are One" is a simple statement of a great soul who perceived life as it really is and not from the mere standpoint of outer conditions.

Taking as the starting point that man has the same life as God, it follows that he uses the same creative process. Everything is one, comes from the same source and returns again to it. "The things which are seen are not made of the things which do appear." What we see comes from what we do not see. This is the explanation of the whole visible universe, and is the only possible explanation.

As God's thought makes worlds and peoples them with all living things, so does our thought make our world and peoples it with all the experiences we have had. By the activity of our thought things come into our life, and we are limited because we have not known the truth; we have thought that outside things controlled us, when all the time we have had that within which could have changed everything and given us freedom from bondage.

The question, then, naturally arises: Why did God create man and *make him a free agent*? If God had created us in such a way as to compel us to do or to be anything that was not of our choosing, we should not have been individuals at all, we should be automatons. Since we know that we are individuals, we know that God made us thus; and we are just discovering the reason why. Let any man wake up to this, the greatest truth in all ages, and he will find it will answer all questions. He will be satisfied that things are what they are.

He will perceive that he may use his own God-given power so to work, to think and to live that he will in no way hinder the greater law from operating *through* him. According to the clearness of his perception and the greatness of his realization of this power will he provide within himself a starting point through which God may operate. There will no longer be a sense of separation, but in its place will come that divine assurance that he is one with God, and thus will he find his freedom from all suffering, whether it be of body, mind or estate.

THE BEGINNING OF UNDERSTANDING

M an is beginning to realize that he has life within him-self as the great gift of God to him. If he really has life, if it is the same nature as the life of God, if he is an individual and has the right of self-choice which constitutes individuality; then it follows that he can do with his life what he wants to do: he can make out of himself that which he wishes. Freedom is his, but this freedom is within law and never outside it. Man must obey law. If he disobeys it, it has to act as law, and so acting has to punish him. This he cannot change but must submit to. Freedom comes to the individual from understanding the laws of his own life, and conforming to them, thereby subjecting them to his use, to the end of health, happiness and success.

Law obtains throughout all nature, governing all things, both the seen and the unseen. Law is not physical or material but mental and spiritual. Law is God's method of operation. We should think of God as the great Spirit whose sole impulse is love, freely giving of Himself to all who ask and refusing none. God is our Father in every sense of the term, watching over, caring for and loving all alike. While all is love, yet, in order that things may not be chaotic, all is governed by law. And as far as you and I are concerned, *this law is always mental.*

OUR CONDITIONS GOVERNED BY OUR THINKING

It is easy for the average person to see how it is that mind can control, and to a certain extent govern, the functions of the body. Some can go even further than this and see that the body is governed entirely by consciousness. This they can see without much difficulty, but it is not so easy for them to see how it is that thought governs their conditions and decides whether they are to be successes or failures.

Here we will stop to ask the question: If our conditions are not controlled by thought, by what, then, are they controlled? Some will say that conditions are controlled by circumstances. But what are circumstances? Are they cause or are they effect? Of course they are always effect; everything that we see is an effect. An effect is something that follows a cause, and we are dealing with causation only; effects do not make themselves, but they are held in place by mind, or causation.

If this does not answer your thought, begin over again and realize that behind everything that is seen is the silent cause. In your life *you are that cause.* There is nothing but Mind, and nothing moves except as Mind moves it. We have agreed that, while God is love, yet your life is governed absolutely by Mind, or Law. In our lives of conditions we are the cause, and nothing moves except as our mind moves it.

The activity of our mind is thought. We are always acting because we are always thinking. At all times we are either drawing things to us or we are pushing them away from us. In the ordinary individual this process goes on without his ever knowing it consciously, but ignorance of the law will excuse no one from its effects.

"What?" someone will say. "Do you think that I thought failure or wanted to fail?" Of course not. You would be foolish to think that; but according to the law which we cannot deny, you must have thought things that would produce failure. Perhaps you thought that failure *might* come, or in some other way you gave it entrance to your mind.

Thinking back over the reason for things, you will find that you are surrounded by a Mind, or Law, that casts back at the thinker, manifested, everything that he thinks. If this were not true, man would not be an individual. Individuality can mean only the ability to think what we *want* to think. If that thought is to have power in our lives then there has to be something that will manifest it. Some are limited and bound by Law through ignorance. This law is sometimes called "Karma," it is the law that binds the ignorant and gives freedom to the wise.

We live in mind; and it can return to us only what we think into it. No matter what we may do, Law will always obtain. If we are thinking of ourselves as poor and needy, then Mind has no choice but to return what we have thought into it. At first this may be hard to realize, but the Truth will reveal to the seeker that Law could act in no other way. Whatever we think is the pattern, and mind is the builder. Jesus, realizing this law, said, "It is done unto you even as you have believed." Shall we doubt but that this great Way Shower knew what he was talking about? Did He not say, "It is done unto you"? What a wonderful thought. "It is done unto you." Nothing to worry about. "It is done unto you." With a tremendous grasp of the power of true spiritual thought, Jesus even called forth bread from the ethers of life, and at no time did He ever fail to demonstrate that when one knows the truth he is freed by that knowledge.

UNCONSCIOUS CREATION

The author once attended a patient who was suffering from a large growth. She was operated on, and about fifty pounds of water were removed. In a few days the growth had returned. Where did it come from? Not from eating or drinking. Neither did it move from one part of the body to another part, as that would not have increased her weight. It must have been created from elements which she took in from the air. It had to come from something not physically seen, something appearing from nothing that we see. What we call "creation" is the same thing—the visible appearing from the invisible. Was not this phenomenon a creation?

Cases as remarkable as this are occurring every day. We should not deny this fact but try to explain it. In the case of this woman there must have been an activity of thought molded forth into form, else how could this growth have appeared? There is nothing manifest but that there is a cause for the manifestation. Investigation proves that behind every condition, whether of body or environment, there has been some thought, conscious or unconscious, which produced that condition. In the case of this woman the thought was not conscious. But creation is going on all the time; we should realize this and learn how to control it so that there may be created for us the things that we desire and not those that we do not want. Is it any wonder that the Bible says, "With all thy getting get understanding"?

Jesus understood all this, and so it was no more effort for Him to do what He did than it is for us to breathe or to digest our food. He *understood*, that is all. Because Jesus did understand and did use these great laws with objective consciousness, people thought He must be God. And when today something unusual occurs, people think that a miracle has been performed. Jesus was not God. He was the manifestation of God; and so are all people. "I say that ye are gods, and every one of you sons of the Most High."

A thinking person will be compelled to admit, in view of all this, that creation is first spiritual, through mental law, and then physical in its manifestation.

Man does not really create. He uses creative power that already is. Relatively speaking, he is the creative power in his own life; and so far as his thought goes, there is something that goes with it that has the power to bring forth into manifestation the thing thought of. Hitherto men have used this creative power in ignorance and so have brought upon themselves all kinds of conditions, but today hundreds of thousands are beginning to use these great laws of their being in a conscious, constructive way. Herein lies the great secret of the New Thought movements under their various names and cults and orders. All are using the same law even though some deny to others the real revelation. We should get into an attitude of mind wherein we recognize the Truth wherever we find it. The trouble with most of us is that unless we see sugar in a sugar bowl we think it must be something else, and so we stick to our petty prejudices instead of looking after principles.

FIRST STEPS

The first thing to realize is that since any thought manifests it necessarily follows that all thought does the same, else how should we know that the particular thought we were thinking would be the one that would create? Mind must cast back all or none. Just as the creative power of the soil receives all seeds put into it, and at once begins to work upon them, so mind must receive all thought and at once begin to operate upon it. Thus we find that all thought has some power in our lives and over our conditions. We are making our environments by the creative power of our thought. God has created us thus and we cannot escape it. By conforming our lives and thought to a greater understanding of Law we shall be able to bring into our experience just what we wish, letting go of all that we do not want to experience and taking in the things we desire.

Every person is surrounded by a thought atmosphere. This mental atmosphere is the direct result of thought which in its turn becomes the direct reason for the cause of that which comes into our lives. Through this power we are either attracting or repelling. Like attracts like and we attract to us just what we are in mind. It is also true that we become attracted to something that is greater than our previous experience by first embodying the atmosphere of our desire.

Every business, every place, every person, everything has a certain mental atmosphere of its own. This atmosphere decides what is to be drawn to it. For instance, you never saw a successful man who went around with an atmosphere of failure. Successful people think about success. A successful man is filled with that subtle something which permeates everything that he does with an atmosphere of confidence and strength. In the presence of some people we feel as though nothing were too great to undertake; we are uplifted; we are inspired to do great things, to accomplish; we feel strong, steady, sure. What a power we feel in the presence of big souls, strong men, noble women!

Did you ever stop to inquire *why* it is that such persons have this kind of an effect over you while others seem to depress, to drag you down, and in their presence you feel as though life were a load to carry? One type is positive, the other negative. In every physical respect they are just alike, but one has a mental and spiritual power which the other does not have, and without that power the individual can hope to do but little.

Which of these two do we like the better? With which do we want to associate? Certainly not with the one that depresses us; we have enough of that already. But what about the man who inspires us with our own worth? Ah, he is the man to whom we will turn every time. Before ever we reach him, in our haste to be near, even to hear his voice, do we not feel a strength coming to meet us? Do you think that this man who has such a wonderful power of attraction will ever want for friends? Will he ever have to look up a position? Already so many positions are open to him that he is weighing in his mind which one to take. He does not have to become a success; he already *is* a success.

Thoughts of failure, limitation or poverty are negative and must be counted out of our lives for all time. Somebody will say, "But what of the poor; what are you going to do with them; are they to be left without help?" No; a thousand times no. The same Power is in them that is in all men. They will always be poor until they awake and realize what life is. All the charity on earth has never done away with poverty, and never will; if it could have done so it would have done so; it could not, therefore it has not. It will do a man a thousand times more good to show him how to succeed than it will to tell him he needs charity. We need not listen to all the calamity howlers. Let them howl if it does them any good.

God has given us a Power and we must use it. We can do more toward saving the world by proving this law than all that charity has ever given it.

Right here, in the manifold world today, there is more money and provision than the world can use. Not even a fraction of the wealth of the world is used. Inventors and discoverers are adding to this wealth every day; they are the real people. But in the midst of plenty, surrounded by all the gifts of heaven, man sits and begs for his daily bread. He should be taught to realize that he has brought these conditions upon himself; that instead of blaming God, man or the devil for the circumstances by which he is surrounded, he should learn to seek the Truth, to let the dead bury their dead. We should tell every man who will believe what his real nature is; show him how to overcome all limitations; give him courage; show him the way. If he will not believe, if he will not walk in the way, it is not our fault, and having done all we can, we must go our way. We may sympathize with *people* but never with trouble, limitation or misery. If people still insist upon hugging their troubles to themselves, all the charity in the world will not help them.

Remember that God is that silent Power behind all things, always ready to spring into expression when we have provided the proper channels, which are receptive and positive faith in the evidence of things not seen with the physical eye but eternal in the heavens.

All is mind, and we must provide a receptive avenue for it as it passes out through us into the outer expression of our affairs. If we allow the world's opinion to control our thinking, then that will be our demonstration. If, on the other hand, we rise superior to the world, we shall do a new thing.

Remember that all people are making demonstrations, only most of them are making the ones they do not desire, but the only ones they can make with their present powers of perception.

HOW TO ATTAIN STRENGTH

Let us see that we use the right attitude of mind in all that we do, filling ourselves with such courage and power of strength that all thought of weakness flees before us. If any thought of weakness should come, ask this question: Is life weak? If life is not weak and if God is not discouraged, then you are not, never were, and never will be. I should like to see the sickly, discouraged thought that could withstand this attitude of mind.

No! Life is strong, and you are strong with the strength of the Infinite; forget all else as you revel in this strength. You are strong and can say I AM. You have been laboring under an illusion; now you are disillusioned. Now you know, and knowing is using the law in a constructive way. "I and my Father are One"; this is strength for the weak, and life for all who believe.

We can so fill ourselves with the drawing power of attraction that it will become irresistible. Nothing can hinder things from coming to the man who knows that he is dealing with the same Power that creates all from itself, moves all within itself, and yet holds all things in their places. I am one with the Infinite Mind. Let this ring through you many times each day until you rise to that height that, looking, sees.

In order to be sure that we are creating the right kind of a mental atmosphere and so attracting what we want, we must at first watch our thinking, lest we create that which we should not like to see manifest. In other words, *we must think only what we wish to experience*. All is mind, and mind casts back at the thinker that only which he thinks. Nothing ever happens by chance. Law governs all life, and all people come under that law. But that law, so far as we are concerned, we ourselves set in motion, and we do this through the power of our thought.

Each person is living in a world of his own making, and he should speak only such words and think only such thoughts as he wishes to see manifested in his life. We must not hear, think, speak, read or listen to limitation of any kind. There is no way under heaven whereby we can think two kinds of thought and get only one result; it is impossible, and the sooner we realize it the sooner we shall arrive. This does not mean that we must be afraid to think lest we create the wrong image, but it does mean that the way most people think can produce nothing but failure; that is why so few succeed.

The person who is to succeed will never let his mind dwell on past mistakes. He will forgive the past in his life and in the lives of other people. If he makes a mistake he will at once forgive it. He will know that so long as he desires any good, there is nowhere in the universe anything that opposes him. God does not damn anyone or anything; man damns everyone and everything.

God does not make things by comparing His power with some other power. God knows that when He speaks it is done; and if we partake of the divine nature we must know the same thing in our lives that God knows in His.

I am the master of my fate,
I am the captain of my soul.

WHAT WE WILL ATTRACT

We will always attract to us, in our lives and conditions, according to our thought. Things are but outer manifestations of inner mental concepts. Thought is not only power; it is also the form of all things. The conditions that we attract will correspond exactly to our mental pictures. It is quite necessary, then, that the successful businessman should keep his mind on thoughts of happiness, which produce cheerfulness instead of depression; he should radiate joy, and should be filled with faith, hope and expectancy. These cheerful, hopeful attitudes of mind are indispensable to the one who really wants to do things in life.

Put every negative thought out of your mind once and for all. Declare your freedom. Know that no matter what others may say, think or do, *you are a success*, now, and nothing can hinder you from accomplishing your good.

All the Power of the Universe is with you; feel it, know it, and then act as though it were true. This mental attitude alone will draw people and things to you.

Begin to blot out, one by one, all false beliefs, all idea that man is limited or poor or miserable. Use that wonderful power of choice that God has given to you. Refuse to think of failure or to doubt your own power.

See only what you wish to experience, and look at nothing else. No matter how many times the old thought returns, destroy it by knowing that it has no power over you; look it squarely in the face and tell it to go; it does not belong to you, and you must know—and stick to it—that you are now free.

Rise up in all the faith of one who knows what he is dealing with, and declare that you are one with Infinite Mind. Know that you cannot get away from this One

Mind; that wherever you may go, there, right beside you, waiting to be used, is all the power there is in the whole universe. When you realize this you will know that in union with this, the only power, *you* are more than all else, *you* are more than anything that can ever happen *to you*.

MORE ABOUT THE POWER OF ATTRACTION

Always remember that Spirit makes things out of itself; it manifests in the visible world by becoming the thing that it wills to become. In the world of the individual the same process takes place. It is given to man to use creative Power, but with the using of this Power comes the necessity of using it as it is made to be used. If God makes things out of His thought before they come into manifestation, then we must use the same method.

You can attract only that which you first mentally become and feel yourself to be in reality, without any doubting. A steady stream of consciousness going out into creative mind will attract a steady manifestation of conditions; a fluctuating stream of consciousness will attract the corresponding manifestation or condition in your life. We must be consistent in our attitude of mind, never wavering. James says, "Ask in faith, nothing doubting, for he that doubteth is like a surge of the sea driven by the wind and tossed. For let not that man think that he shall receive anything of the Lord."

We are all immersed in an aura of our own thinking. This aura is the direct result of all that we have ever said, thought or done; it decides what is to take place in our life; it attracts what is like itself and repels what is unlike itself. We are drawn toward those things that we mentally embody. Most of the inner processes of thought have been unconscious; but when we understand the Law all that we have to do is to embody consciously what we wish, and think of that only, and then we shall be drawn silently toward it.

We have this Law in our hands to do with as we will. We can draw what we want only as we let go of the old order and take up the new; and this we must do to the exclusion of all else. This is no weak man's job but an undertaking for a strong, self-reliant soul; and the end is worth the effort. The person who can keep his thoughts one-pointed is the one who will obtain the best results.

But this does not imply the necessity of strain or anything of a strenuous nature; on the contrary, strain is just what we must avoid. When we know that there is but one Power we shall not struggle, we shall know, and in calmness we shall see only what we know must be the Truth. This means a persistent, firm determination to think what we want to think, regardless of all outer evidence to the contrary. We look not to the seen but to the unseen. The king of Israel understood this when, looking upon the advancing host of the enemy, he said, "We have no might against this great company, but our eyes are upon Thee"—upon the One Power.

HOW TO ATTRACT FRIENDS

The man who has learned to love all people, no matter who they may be, will find plenty of people who will return that love to him. This is not mere sentiment, and it is more than a religious attitude of mind; it is a deep scientific fact, and one to which we should pay attention. The reason is this: As all is Mind, and as we attract to us what we first become, until we learn to love we are not sending out love vibrations, and not until we send out love vibrations can we receive love in return.

One of the first things to do is to learn to love everybody. If you have not done this, begin to do so at once. There is always more good than bad in people, and seeing the good tends to bring it forth. Love is the greatest healing and drawing power on earth. It is the very reason for our being, and that explains why it is that people should have something or somebody to love.

The life that has not loved has not lived; it is still dead. Love is the sole impulse for creation; and the man who does not have it as the greatest incentive in his life has never developed the real creative instinct. No one can swing out into the Universal without love, for the whole universe is based upon it.

When we find that we are without friends, the thing to do is at once to send our thought out to the whole world—send it full of love and affection. Know that this thought will meet the desires of some other person who is wanting the same thing, and in some way the two will be drawn together. Get over thinking that people are queer. That kind of thought will only produce misunderstanding and cause us to lose the friends that we now have. Think of the whole world as your friend; but you must also be the friend of the whole world. In this way and with this simple practice you will draw to you so many friends that the time will be too short to enjoy them all. Refuse to see the negative side of anyone. Refuse to let yourself misunderstand or be misunderstood. Do not be morbid. Know that everyone wants you to have the best; affirm this wherever you go and then you will find things just as you wish them to be.

The atmosphere created by a real lover of the race is so powerful that although his other shortcomings may be many, still the world will love him in return. "To him who loveth much, much will be forgiven." People are dying for real human interest, for someone to tell them that they are all right. Which person do we like the better: the one who is always full of trouble and faultfinding, or the one who looks at the world as his friend and loves it? The question does not need to be asked; we know that we want the company of the person who loves and loving, forgets all else.

The only reason we think other people are "queer" is because they do not happen to think as we do. We must get over this little, petty attitude and see things in the large.

The person who sees what he wants to see, regardless of what appears, will some day experience in the outer what he has so faithfully seen within.

From selfish motives alone, if from no loftier reason, we cannot afford to find fault or to hate or even to hold in mind anything against any living soul. The God who is love cannot hear the prayer of the man who is not love. Love and co-operation will yet be found to be the greatest business principle on earth. "God is Love."

We will make our unity with all people, with all life. We will affirm that God in us is unified with God in all. This One is now drawing into our life all love and fellowship. I am one with all people, with all things, with all life. As I listen in the silence the voice of all humanity speaks to me and answers the love that I hold out to it.

This great love that I now feel for the world is the love of God, and it is felt by all and returned from all. Nothing comes in between because there is nothing but love to come in between. I understand all people and that understanding is reflected back to me from all people. I help, therefore I am helped. I uplift, therefore I am uplifted. Nothing can mar this perfect picture of myself and my relations with the world; it is the truth, the whole truth, and nothing but the truth. I am now surrounded by all love, all friendship, all companionship, all health, all happiness, all success. I am one with life. I wait in the silence while the Great Spirit bears this message to the whole world.

THE CONTROL OF THOUGHT

The man who can control his thought can have and do what he wishes to have and to do; everything is his for the asking. He must remember that whatever he gets is his to use but not his to hold. Creation is always flowing by and we have as much of it as we can take and use; more would cause stagnation.

We are relieved of all thought of clinging to anybody or anything. Cannot the Great Principle of Life create for us faster than we can spend or use? The universe is inexhaustible; it is limitless; it knows no bounds and has no confines. We are not depending on a reed shaken by the wind, but on the *principle of life itself*, for all that we want, have or ever shall have. It is not *some* power, or *a great* power, we affirm again; it is ALL POWER. All that we have to do is to believe this and act as though it were so, never wavering, not even once, no matter what happens. As we do this we shall find that things are steadily coming our way, and that they are coming without that awful effort that destroys the peace of the majority of the race. We know that there can be no failure in the Divine Mind, and this Mind is the Power on which we are depending.

Now just because we are depending upon Divine Mind we must not think that we do not have to do our share. God will work through us if we will let Him, but we must act in the outer as though we were sure of ourselves. Our part is to believe, and then to act in faith.

Jesus went to the tomb of Lazarus believing and knowing that God was working through Him. Often we may have to go somewhere or do something and we must know with deep conviction that there will be a power going with us that none can gainsay. When we feel this secure place in our thought, all that we will have to do is to act. There is no doubt but that the *creative power of the universe will answer; it always does*. And so we need not take the worry upon ourselves, but rather we will "Make known our requests with thanksgiving."

When Jesus said, "All things whatsoever ye pray and ask for, believe that ye receive them and ye shall have them," he was uttering one of those many deep truths that were so clear to Him and that we are just beginning to see. He knew that everything is made out of Mind and that without that positive acceptance on the part of the individual there is no mold into which Mind can pour itself forth into form. In the Mind of God there is the correct mold, the true knowing, but in the mind of man there is not always this true knowing. Since God can do *for* us only by doing *through* us, nothing can be done for us unless we are positively receptive, but when we realize the law and how it works, then we will provide that complete inner acceptance. By so doing we permit the Spirit to do the work, to make the gift.

The reason we can make our requests known with thanksgiving is because we know from the beginning that we are to receive and therefore we cannot help being thankful. This grateful attitude to the Spirit puts us in very close touch with power and adds much to the reality of the thing that we are dealing with. Without it we can do but little. So let us cultivate all the gratitude that we can. In gratitude we will send our thoughts out into the world, and as it comes back it will come laden with the fruits of the Spirit.

CREATING ATMOSPHERE

To the student who has realized that all is Mind and that everything is governed by Law, there comes another thought: it is that he can create, or have created for him, from his own thinking. He can create such a strong mental atmosphere of success that its power of attraction will be irresistible. He can send his thought throughout the world and have it bring back to him whatever he wants. He can so fill his place of business with the power of success that it will draw from far and near. Thought will always bring back to us what we send out. First we must clear our thought of all unbelief. This book is written for those who believe; and to those who do believe it will come true in their lives.

Without mental clearness on the part of the thinker there can be no real creative work done. As water will reach only its own level, so Mind will return to us only what we first believe. We are always getting what we believe but not always what we want. Our thought has the power to reach, in the outer form of conditions, an exact correspondence to our inner convictions.

By thinking, you set in motion a Power that creates. It will be exactly as you think. You throw out into Mind an idea, and Mind creates It for you and sets It on the path of your life. Think of It, then, as your greatest friend. It is always with you wherever you may be. It never deserts you. You are never alone. There is no doubt, no fear, no wondering; you *know*. You are going to use the only Power that there is in the Universe. You are going to use it for a definite purpose. You have already fixed this purpose in your thought; now you are going to speak it forth.

You are speaking it for your own good. You desire only the good and you know that only the good can come to you. You have made your unity with life, and now life is going to help you in your affairs.

You are going to establish in your rooms such an atmosphere of success that it will become an irresistible power; it will sweep everything before it as it realizes the greatness and the All-Mightiness of the One. You are so sure, that you will not even look to see if it is going to happen; you KNOW.

And now your word, which is one with the Infinite Life, is to be spoken in calm, perfect trust. It is to be taken up, and at once it is to be operated on. Perfect is the pattern and perfect will be the result. You see yourself surrounded by the thing that you desire. More than this, you *are* the thing that you desire. Your word is now establishing it forever; see this, feel it, know it. You are now encompassed by perfect life, by infinite activity, by all power, by all guidance. The power of the Spirit is drawing to you all people; it is supplying you with all good; it is filling you with all life, truth and love.

Wait in perfect silence while that inner power takes it up. And then you know that it is done unto you. There goes forth from this word the power of the Infinite. "The words which I speak, they are spirit and they are life."

THE POWER OF WORDS

Man's word, spoken forth into Creative Mind, is endowed with power of expression. "By our words we are justified and by our words we are condemned." Our word has the exact amount of power that we put into it. This does not mean power through effort or strain but power through absolute conviction, or faith. It is like a little messenger who knows what he is doing and knows just how to do it. We speak into our words the intelligence which we are, and backed by that greater intelligence of the Universal Mind our word becomes a law unto the thing for which it is spoken. Jesus understood this far better than we do. Indeed, He absolutely believed it, for He said, "Heaven and earth shall pass away but my words shall not pass away till all be fulfilled."

This makes our word inseparable from Absolute Intelligence and Power. Now if any word has power it must follow that all words have power. Some words may have a greater power than others, according to our conviction, but all words have some power. How careful, then, we should be what kind of words we are speaking.

All this goes to prove that we really are one with the Infinite Mind, and that our words have the power of life within them; that the word is always with us and never far off. The word is within our own mouth. Every time we speak we are using power.

We are one in Mind with the whole universe; we are all eternally united in this Mind with real power. It is our own fault if we do not use this truth after we see it. We should feel ourselves surrounded by this Mind, this great pulsating life, this all-seeing and all-knowing reality. When we do feel this near presence, this great power and life, then all we have to do is to speak forth into it, speak with all the positive conviction of the soul that has found its source, and above all else never fear but that it will be done unto us even as we have believed.

What wonderful power, what a newness of life and of power of expression, is waiting for those who really believe. What may the race not attain to when men wake up to the real facts of being? As yet the race has not begun to live, but the time is drawing near. Already thousands are using this great Power, and thousands are eagerly watching and waiting for the new day.

WHY BELIEF IS NECESSARY

Always when we pray we must believe. Our idea of prayer is not so much asking God for things as it is believing that we already have the things that we need. As we have said before, this *already believing* is necessary because all is Mind, and until we have provided that full acceptance we have not made a mold into which mind could pour itself and through which it could manifest. This positive belief is absolutely essential to real creative work; and if we do not at present have it, then we must develop it.

All is law, and cause and effect obtain through all life. Mind is cause, and what we term matter, or the visible, is effect. As water will freeze into the form that it is poured, so mind will solidify only into the forms that our thought takes. Thought is form. The individual provides the form; he never creates or even manifests, that is, of himself; there is something that does all this for him. His sole activity is the use of this Power. This Power is always at hand ready to be spoken into and at once ready to form the words into visible expression. But the mold that most of us provide is a very poor one, and we change it so quickly that it is more like a motion picture than anything else.

Already we have the Power; it is the gift of the Most High in its Finite Expression. But our ignorance of its use has caused us to create the wrong form, which in its turn has caused Mind to produce the form which we have thought into it. From this Law of Cause and Effect we may never hope to escape; and while we may think of it as a hard thing, at first, yet, when we understand, we shall see it as absolute justice without which there could be no real self-acting, individual life at all. Because of our Divine individuality, even God may have to wait our recognition of Him and His laws.

People in business will do well to remember this and so to form their thought that they will be willing to receive what they send out. No thought of discouragement or disorder should ever be created, but only positive assurance, strong thoughts of success, of Divine activity, the feeling that with God all things are possible, the belief that we are One with that Great Mind. These are the thoughts that make for success.

The realization that we are dealing with one and not with two powers enables us to think with clearness. We are not troubled about competition or opposition or failure because there is nothing but life, and this life is continually giving to us all that we could ask for, wish, or think into it.

We can now see how essential it is that thought should be held one-pointed; that we should think always and only upon what we want, never letting our mind dwell on anything else. In this way the Spirit works through us.

WHERE SO MANY FAIL

The ordinary individual, sitting down to give a treatment to his business, unconsciously does just the thing that he should have avoided; and then he wonders why he did not get the desired results. Most people simply sit and wish for, or long for, something. They may even have a great desire or hope. They may even go so far as to believe that their desire is going to happen. All this is good as far as it goes, but it does not go far enough. What we must do is to provide that already-having-received attitude. This may seem hard at first but we can easily see that it is necessary; and as it is the only way that mind works, this is what we must do.

Power is, and Mind is, and life is; but they have to flow through us in order to express in our lives. We are dealing with law; and nature must be obeyed before it will work for us. Just realize that this law is as natural a law as any other of God's laws, and use it with the same intelligence that you would use the law of electricity; then you will get the desired results. We provide the thought form around which the divine energies play and to which they attract the conditions necessary for the fulfillment of the thought.

When we give a treatment this is all that we have to do, but before we can do even this we have to clear our minds of all fear, of every sense of separation from the Divine Mind. Law is; but we must enforce it, or use it, in our own lives. Nothing can happen to us that is not first an accepted belief in our own consciousness. We may not always be aware of what is going on within, but practice will enable us to control our thought more and more so that we shall be able to think what we want to think, regardless of what may seem to be the case.

Each person has within himself the capacity of knowing and making use of the law but it must be consciously developed. This is done by practice, and by willingness to learn and to utilize whatever we know so far as we have gone.

The individual who has the most power is the one who has the greatest realization of the Divine Presence, and to whom this means the most as an active principle of his life.

We all need more backbone and less wishbone. There is something which waits only our recognition to spring into being, bringing with it all the Power in the universe.

USING THE IMAGINATION

Just imagine yourself surrounded by Mind, so plastic, so receptive, that it receives the slightest impression of your thought. Whatever you think it takes up and executes for you. Every thought is received and acted upon. Not some but all thoughts. Whatever the pattern we provide, that will be our demonstration. If we cannot get over thinking that we are poor then we will still remain poor. As soon as we become rich in our thought then we will be rich in our expression. These are not mere words, but the deepest truth that has ever come to the human race. Hundreds of thousands of the most intelligent thinkers and the most spiritual people of our day are proving this truth. We are not dealing with illusions but with realities; pay no more attention to the one who ridicules these ideas than you would to the blowing of the wind.

In the center of your own soul choose what you want to become, to accomplish; keep it to yourself. Every day in the silence of absolute conviction know that it is now done. It is just as much done, as far as *you* are concerned, as it will be when you experience it in the outer. Imagine yourself to be what you want to be. See only that which you desire, refuse even to think of the other. Stick to it, never doubt. Say many times a day, "I am that thing," realize what this means. It means that the great Universal power of Mind *is* that, and it cannot fail.

MAN'S RIGHT OF CHOICE

Man is created an individual, and as such he has the power of choice. Many people seem to think that man should not choose, that since he has asked the Spirit to lead him, he need no longer act, or choose. This is taught by many teachers but is not consistent with our individuality. Unless we had this privilege, this power of choice, we would not be individuals. What we *do* need to learn is that the Spirit can choose through us. But when this happens it is an act on our part. Even though we say, "I will not choose," we are still choosing; because we are choosing not to choose.

We cannot escape the fact that we are made in such a way that at every step life is a constant choice. What we do need to do is to select what we feel to be right and know that the universe will never deny us anything. We choose and Mind creates. We should endeavor to choose that which will express always a greater life and we must remember that the Spirit is always seeking to express love and beauty through us. If we are attuned to these, and are working in harmony with the great creative power, we need have no doubt about its willingness to work for us.

We must know exactly what it is that we wish and get the perfect mental picture of it. We must believe absolutely that we now have it and never do or say anything that denies it.

OLD AGE AND OPPORTUNITY

One of the besetting errors of people is a belief that they are too old to do things. This comes from a lack of understanding what life really is. Life is consciousness and not years. The man or woman who is seventy years old should be better able to demonstrate than the man who is only twenty. He should have evolved a higher thought, and it is thought and not conditions that we are dealing with.

Amelia Barr was fifty-three before she wrote a book. After that she wrote over eighty, all of which had a large circulation. Mary Baker Eddy was sixty before she began her work, and she attended to all of her great activities until she passed from this plane to a higher one. The author of this book once took a man who was over sixty, one who thought his chance for success had gone, and through teaching him these principles in a year's time made him a prosperous businessman. He is now doing well and was never before in his life so happy. The last time he was interviewed he said that business was increasing every day and that he had not begun yet. Every day he stands in his store and claims more activity. He speaks the word and realizes increase all the time. If this were not true then life would not be worth the living. What is a few years in eternity? We must get over these false notions about age and competition. In the truth the word competition is never mentioned. The people who think about it have never known the truth.

Life is what we make it from within and never from without. We are just as old as we think we are, no matter what the number of years may have been that we have lived on this planet.

DEMONSTRATING SUCCESS
IN BUSINESS

All demonstrations take place within ourselves. Creation is eternally flowing through all things. The law is always working from that inner pattern. We do not struggle with conditions, we use principles which create conditions. What we can mentally encompass we can accomplish, no matter how hard it may seem from the outside.

All external things are but the outer rim of inner thought activity. You can easily prove this for yourself. If you are in business, say, running an ice cream stand or counter, and are not doing good business, look carefully into your own thought and see what you will find. You will find that it is an established belief there that business is not good. You are not feeling a sense of activity. You will not find within your thought any feeling of success. You are not expecting many customers.

Now suppose someone comes along and says to you: "What is the matter? Why are you not doing more business?" This is about what the answer would be: "People don't seem to want what I have to sell." Or perhaps something like this: "I am too old to compete with modern methods." Or even: "Well, times are hard." All this is negative thought.

Now this man to whom you are talking does not believe a word you have said. He knows that causation is in mind and not in matter, and he says: "The whole thing is in your own mind; the trouble with you is that you don't feel that you are a success."

Perhaps you have heard something of this before; if so you will ask him what he means, or perhaps you think he is talking about something peculiar; but we are taking it for granted that you are so anxious to do something to make your business a success that you will be willing to try anything, so you ask him to explain. He begins by telling you all is Mind; nothing moves but Mind moves it and that you are a center in this Mind. You do not understand how this relates in any way to your business, but he goes on to say that your thought decides whether your business shall be a success or a failure. Here you become indignant, and ask if he means to tell you that you want to fail. Of course he knows you do not, and he explains that while you wish success, you are thinking failure, fearing it, and that there is a law that makes your thought, never asking questions but at once sets about its fulfillment. You become interested and ask how this can be; in return you are asked this question: "How did anything come into being?" This sets you to thinking and of course you realize that there was a time when nothing existed but life; so whatever has come into being must have come from that life, for what we see must come from that which we do not see. You have to admit that. Then what you do not see must be the Cause of everything; and you must also admit that; and that Cause works by Law; this you are compelled to admit. Then this Law, being everywhere, must be in you; this is harder for you to see; but after much thought you begin to realize that it is so. Then you, without knowing where your thought processes were leading you, have conceded that you, yourself, are the reason for what happens in your life, be it success or failure.

God couldn't make you any other way and at the same time make you a self-choosing individual. This is plain.

Now what are you going to do about it? This is what you must do. For every time that you have thought failure you are going to replace it with strong radiant thoughts of success. You are going to speak activity into your business. You are going daily to see nothing but activity and to know that it is Law that you are using, Universal Law, and as such your thought is as sure as the thought of God.

Daily you are going to give to the Great Creative Mind exactly what you want to happen. You will see only what you desire and in the silence of your soul you will speak and it will be done unto you. You will come to believe that a great Divine Love flows through you and your affairs. You will be grateful for this Love.

It fills your life. It satisfies your soul. You are a different man. You are so filled with activity and courage that when you meet people they will wonder at your energy. They will begin to wish simply to come in contact with you. They will feel uplifted.

In the course of a few months you will be a success. People will come to you and say: "How do you do it?" The answer will be the same that was given to you a few months ago.

Let the man who is speaking to the public do the same thing. Let him daily see throngs of people coming to hear him. Let him see nothing else. He will experience what he feels, and sees.

Always remember this. *Life is from within outward, and never from without inward.* You are the center of power in your own life.

Be sure and not take on false suggestion. The world is full of calamity howlers; turn from them, every one, no matter how great you think they may be; you haven't the time to waste over anything that is negative. You *are* a success, and you are giving to the Law, every day, just what you want done. And the Law is always working for you. All fear has gone and you know that there is but One Power in all the Universe. Happy is the man who knows this, the greatest of all Truths.

The whole thing resolves itself into our mental ability to control our thought. The man who can do this, can *have* what he wants, can *do* what he wishes, and *becomes* what he wills. Life, God, the Universe, is his.

MONEY A SPIRITUAL IDEA

M any people seem to think that money must be evil, but actually it is only an inordinate love of money that is characterized as the "root of all evil."

If *all* is an expression of life, then *money* is an expression of life, and as such, must be good. Without a certain amount of it in this life, we would have a hard time. But how to get it; that is the race problem. How shall we acquire wealth? Money didn't make itself, and not being self-creative it must be an effect. Behind it must be the Cause that projects it. That cause is never seen; no cause is ever seen. Consciousness is cause and people who have a money consciousness have the outward expression of it. People who have it as a sure reality in their mind, have it as an expression in their pocket. People who don't have this mental likeness don't have money in their pockets.

What we need to do is to acquire a money consciousness. This may seem very material, but the true idea of money is not material—it is spiritual. We need to make our unity with it. We can never do this while we hold it away from us by thinking that we haven't it. Let us change the method and begin to make our unity with supply by daily declaring that all the Power in the Universe is daily bringing to us all that we can use. Feel the presence of supply. Know that it is yours now.

Make yourself feel that you now have, and to you shall be given. Work with yourself until there is nothing in you that doubts. Money can not be kept away from the man who understands that all is Mind, and that Divine Law governs his life.

Daily give thanks for perfect supply. Feel it to be yours, that you have entered into the full possession of it now.

Refuse to talk poverty or limitation. Stick to it that you are rich. Get the million-dollar consciousness. There is no other way, and this will react into everything that you do.

See money coming to you from every source and from every direction. Know that everything is working for your good.

Realize in your life the presence of an Omnipotent Power. Speak forth into It, and feel that It responds to your approach.

Whenever you see anything or anybody whom you think

has more than you, at once affirm that you have the same thing. This doesn't mean that you have what is his, but that you have as much. It means that all you need is yours.

Whenever you think about anything big, at once say, "That means me." In this way you learn to unify yourself, in the Law, with large concepts, and according to the way that Law works, it will tend to produce that thing for you.

Never let yourself doubt for even a minute. Always be positive about yourself. Keep watch over the inner workings of your thought, and the Law will do the rest.

ACTION

The Universe is teeming with activity. There is motion everywhere. Nothing ever stands still. All activity comes from Mind. If we want to be in line with things we must move. This doesn't mean that we must strain or struggle, but we must be willing to do our part by letting the Law work through us.

God can do for us only as we will allow Him to do through us. Intelligence gives us ideas and in our turn we work on them. But our work is no longer done in any sense of doubt or fear, for we know that we are dealing with something that never makes a mistake. We proceed with a calm confidence born of the inner trust in a Power that is Infinite.

Behind all of our movements, then, is a great purpose, to let the Law work through us.

We must comply with the Law of Activity. We must be willing to take the way of outer activity. Jesus went to the tomb of Lazarus. We may have to go but there will accompany us something that never fails.

This Law of Activity we must use in our business. So many business places that we go into have such an atmosphere of inactivity, produce such a drowsy feeling, that we at once lose all interest in what is going on. We don't feel like buying. We leave that place without any apparent reason and go into another. Here we feel that all is life, all is motion, all is activity. We feel confident that this is the place we are looking for. We will buy here; we find just what we want; we are satisfied with our purchase and go away cheerful.

Now to create this activity something more than thought is essential. Not that it does not come first, but the one who has this thought of activity will naturally manifest it in vigorous, energetic movement which helps to produce a spirit of activity in his business and in everything he undertakes. Wherever you see a man who does not move, then you will find one whose thought is inactive; the two always go together.

A man in a store or place of business should always be moving his goods. He should always be doing something.

People will see this and getting the thought of activity behind it will want to trade there. We are not attracted to a store that always has the same things on the same shelf. The world likes action, change. Action is Life.

Let a clerk in a store think activity and begin to manifest it, even though he may not be waiting on customers, and in a short time he will be waiting on them. Alertness is the word. Always be alert. *There must be mental alertness before there can be physical activity*.

Act as though things were happening even though they may not appear to be. Keep things moving and soon you will have to avoid the rush. Activity is genius. Half the stores that you go into make you sleepy before you get out, and you feel as though you can't get out fast enough. The other half are alive and those are the ones who are doing the business of the world.

The man who is active in his thought doesn't have to sit by himself to think; he works while he thinks and so complies with the Law which has to work through him. The thought of activity makes him move, and the thought of confidence makes his movements sure, and the thought of Supreme Guidance makes his work intelligent.

We must be careful and not get into ruts; always be doing something new and different, and you will find life becomes a great game in which you are taking the leading part.

Life will never become tiresome to the active mind and body. It is so interesting that we wonder if we will ever get enough of it. Some people get into such lazy mental habits that a new idea cannot find entrance. Great things are done by people who think great thoughts and then go out into the world to make their dreams come true.

If you can't find anything new to do, go home and change the bed around, or the piano; put the cook stove in the parlor and eat on the back step for a time. It will start something moving and changing in you that will never stop. The wide-awake person can find so many things to do that he hasn't time even to begin in this life, and he knows that Eternity is necessary to carry out the ideals that he already has evolved.

Everything comes from Mind, but Mind acts on itself, and we must act on ourselves and on conditions; not as a slave but as a master. Be interested in life, if you want life to be interested in you. Act in Life, and Life will act through you. So will you also become one of the great people on earth.

IDEAS OF THE INFINITE

S uppose that we wish to draw from the Universal Mind some definite idea, some guidance, some information, some leading. How are we going to do this? First we must become convinced that we can do it.

Where do all the inventions come from? Where does Edison get his information about electricity? Where, if not direct from the Mind of the Universe? Everything that has ever come into the race comes direct from Mind.

It could come from nothing else.

Every invention is but a discovery of something that already is, although we may not have seen it. Where does the harmony of music come from? Where could it originate except in Mind? Does not a great musician listen and hear something that we do not hear? His ear is attuned to Harmony, and he catches it straight from Life itself and interprets it to the world. We are surrounded by the music of the spheres, but few of us ever catch the sound.

We are so filled with trouble that the Divine Melody is never heard. If we could see, if we could hear, if we could understand, if we only realized the presence of the All, what could we not do?

When a great thought springs up in the mind of an individual, when a great poem is written, when a great work of art is wrought by some receptive artist, it is simply a sign that the veil is thin between; he has caught a glimpse of reality.

But for most of us Inspiration is not to be depended on, and we must take the slower but nonetheless sure method of receiving straight from the Infinite. The method is a simple one, and very effective. When you want to know a certain thing, or how to begin a certain line of action:

First, you must be quiet within yourself. You must not be confused by any outward appearance. Never become disturbed by effects. They didn't make themselves and have no intelligence to contradict you.

Be quiet until you realize the presence of absolute Intelligence all around you, of the Mind that knows. Now get a perfect picture of just what you desire. You cannot get a picture unless you know what it is you want. Put your mind in touch with Universal Mind, saying just what you are waiting for. Ask for it, believe that you are receiving it, and wait. After a few minutes declare that you now know, even though you may not seem to know, yet in the depths of consciousness you have received the impression. Give thanks that you now receive. Do this every day until you get some direction. It is sometimes a good thing to do this just before going to sleep.

Never, after you have done this, deny the knowledge that

has been given you. The time will come when some idea will begin to take form. Wait for it and, when it does appear, act upon it with all the conviction of one who is perfectly sure of himself.

You have gotten understanding straight from the source of all understanding, knowledge from the source of knowledge. All can do this if they will be persistent. It is a sure direction and guidance and will never fail us. But we must be sure that we are not denying in other moments what we affirm in the moments of Faith. In this way we will make fewer mistakes and in time our lives will be controlled by supreme wisdom and understanding.

DON'T BE A LEANER

Never lean on other people. You have strength of your own that is great enough to do all that is necessary. The Almighty has implanted genius within the soul of everyone and what we need to do is to unearth that inner genius and cause it to shine forth. We will never do this while we look to others for guidance. "To thine own self repair, wait thou within the silence dim, and thou shalt find Him there."

All the power and intelligence of the Universe is already

within, waiting to be utilized. The Divine Spark must be fanned into a blaze of the living Fire of your own divinity.

Self-reliance is the word to dwell on. Listen to your own voice; it will speak in terms that are unmistakable. Trust in your own self more than in all else. All great men have learned to do this. Every person, within his soul, is in direct communication with the Infinite Understanding. When we depend on other people we are simply taking their light and trying to light our path with it. When we depend on ourselves we are depending on that inner voice that is God, speaking in and through man. "Man is the inlet and the outlet to all there is in God." God has made us and brought us up to where we recognize our own individuality; from now on we will have to let Him express through us. If it were different we should not be individuals. "Behold I stand at the door and wait." This is a statement of the near presence of power; but we, the Individual, must open the door. This door is our thought and we are the guardian of it, and when we do open the door we will find that the Divine Presence is right at hand, waiting, ready and willing to do for us all that we can believe.

We are strong with the strength of the Infinite. We are not weak. We are great and not mean. We are One with the Infinite Mind.

When you have a real thing to do, keep it to yourself.

Don't talk about it. Just know in your own mind what it is that you want and keep still about it. Often when we think that we will do some big thing we begin to talk about it and the first thing we know all the power seems to be gone.

This is what happens. We are all sending out into Mind a constant stream of thought; the clearer it is, the better will it manifest; if it becomes doubtful it will not have so clear a manifestation. If it is confused it will manifest only confusion. All this is according to the Law of Cause and Effect, and we cannot change that Law. Too often, when we tell our friends what we are going to do, they confuse our thought by laughing about it, or by doubting our capacity to do so large a thing. Of course this would not happen if we were always positive, but when we become the least bit negative it will react and we will lose that power of clearness which is absolutely necessary to good creative work.

When you want to do a big thing, get the mental pattern, make it perfect, know just what it means, enlarge your thought, keep it to yourself, pass it over to the creative power behind all things, wait and listen, and when the impression comes, follow it with assurance. *Don't talk to anyone about it*. Never listen to negative talk or pay any attention to it and you will succeed where all others fail.

CAUSES AND CONDITIONS

When we realize that life is not fundamentally physical, but mental and spiritual, it will not be hard for us to see that by a certain mental and spiritual process we can demonstrate what we want.

We are not dealing with conditions but with causes. Causes originate only from the unseen side of life. This is not strange as the same might be said of electricity, or even of life itself. We do not see life, we only see what it does. This we call a condition. Of itself it is simply an effect. We are living in the outer world of effects and in the inner world of causes. These causes we set in motion by our thought, and, through the power inherent within the cause, expresses the thought as a condition. It follows that the cause must be equal to the effect and that the effect always evaluates with the cause held in mind. Everything comes from One Substance, and our thought qualifies that Substance and determines what is to take place in our life.

The whole teaching of the *Bhagavad Gita* is that there is but One and that it becomes to us just what we first believe into it. In other words we manifest the unmanifested. This in no way takes away from the omnipotence of God, but adds to it, for He has created something that is able to do this. God still rules in the Universe, but we are given the power to rule in our lives.

We must realize, then, absolutely that we are dealing with a Substance with which we have a right to deal, and by learning its laws we will be able to subject them to our use, just as Edison does with electricity. Law *is*, but we must use it.

The substance that we deal with, in itself, is never limited, but we often are, because we draw only what we believe.

Because we are limited is no reason why the Universe should have limitation. Our limitation is only our unbelief; life can give us a big thing or a little thing. When it gives us a little thing, it is not limited, any more than life is limited when it makes a grain of sand, because it could just as well have made a planet. But in the great scheme of things all kinds of forms, small and large, are necessary, which, combined, make a complete whole. The power and substance behind everything remain Infinite.

Now this life can become to us only through us, and that becoming is the passing of Spirit into expression in our lives through the form of the thought that we give to it. In itself life is never limited; an ant has just as much life as an elephant though smaller in size. The question is not one of size but one of consciousness.

We are not limited by actual boundaries, but by false

ideas about life and by a failure to recognize that we are dealing with the Infinite.

Limitation is an experience of the race, but it is not the fault of God, it is the fault of man's perception. And to prove that this is so, let any man break the bonds of this false sense of life and he at once begins to express less and less limitation. It is a matter of the growth of the inner idea.

People often say when they are told this, "Do you think that I decided to be poor and miserable; do you take me for a fool?" No, you are not a fool, but it is quite possible that you have been fooled, and most of us have been. I know of no one who has escaped being fooled about life; you may not have had thoughts of poverty but at the same time you may have had thoughts that have produced it. Just watch the process of your thinking and see how many times a day you think something that you would not want to happen. This will satisfy you that you need to be watchful, that your thought needs to be controlled.

What we need to do is to reverse the process of our thinking and see to it that we think only positive, constructive thoughts. A calm determination to think just what we want to think regardless of conditions will do much to put us on the highway to a greater realization of life.

Of course we will fall, of course the road is not easy, but

we will be growing. Daily we will be giving to the Creative Mind a newer and a greater concept to be worked out into the life around us. Daily we will be overcoming some negative tendency. We must stick to it until we gain the mastery of all our thought and in that day we will rise never to fall again.

We must be good-natured with ourselves, never becoming discouraged or giving up until we overcome. Feel that you are always backed by an Omnipotent power and a kind Father of Love, and the way will become easier.

MENTAL EQUIVALENTS

One of the most important things to remember is that we cannot demonstrate life beyond our mental ability to embody. We give birth to an idea only from within ourselves. What we are, we put into our thinking. What we are not, we cannot put into it.

If we are to draw from Life what we want, we must first think it forth into Life. It always produces what we think. In order to have success, we must first conceive it in our own thought. This is not because we are creators, but because the flow of Life into manifestation, through us, must take the form we give to it, and if we want a thing we must have within ourselves the mental equivalent before we get it.

This is what Jesus meant when he said that we must believe when we pray. This belief is providing within us that something which knows before it sees what it asks for.

For instance, suppose a man is praying for activity (our idea of prayer is the accepting of a thing before we get it) in his affairs. First, before this activity can come, he must have it within himself; he must come to see activity in everything; there must be something that corresponds to the thing that he wants; he must have a mental equivalent.

We find that we attract to ourselves as much of anything as we embody within. As water will reach only its own level, so our outward conditions will re-produce only our inner realizations.

A man will always draw to him just what he is. But we can learn to provide within the image of what we desire and so in a definite way use the law to get just what we need. If at first we do not have a great realization of activity we will have to work on what we do have, and as our outer conditions come up to meet the inner cause, we will find that it will be much easier to enlarge the inner receptivity for something greater and more worthwhile. Of one thing we may be assured—we must all start somewhere, and that somewhere is within ourselves. In this *within* we must make the affirmation, and there, too, we must do the real work of realization. At the first the way may seem hard, for we are constantly confronted with that which seems to be, and we are not always sure of ourselves nor strong enough to overcome, but we may rest content in the assurance that we are growing. Every day we will be providing a bigger concept of life, and with the inner growth we will have an enlarged power to speak forth into the Creative Mind, with the result that we shall get a fresh impulse and be doing a bigger thing for ourselves. Growth and realization are always from within and never from without.

The old race suggestion of fear and poverty and limitation must be done away with and daily we must clear our thought from all that limits the One from showing forth in our life.

Remember that you are dealing with One power, and not with two. This will make it easier, for you do not have to overcome any condition, because conditions flow from within out, and not from without in.

A man going to a new town will at once begin to attract to him just what he brings in his thought. He should be very careful what he thinks. He should know just what he wants and daily give it over to the Supreme Mind, knowing that It will work for him. Old thoughts must be destroyed, and new must take their places. Every time the old thought comes look it squarely in the face and declare that it has no part in your mind. It has no power over you. You state the Law and rely on it to the exclusion of all else. Daily try to see more and to understand more, feel every day that you are being especially looked after. There is no special creation for any individual, but we all specialize the Law every time we think into it. For all our thought is taken up and something is always done with it.

A good practice is to sit and realize that you are a center of Divine attraction, that all things are coming to you, that the power within is going out and drawing back all that you will ever need. Don't argue about it, just do it, and when you have finished leave it all to the Law, knowing that it will be done. Declare that all life, all love and power are now in your life. Declare that you are now in the midst of plenty. Stick to it even though you may not as yet see the result. It will work and those who believe the most always get the most. Think of the Law as your friend, always looking out for your interest. Trust completely in it and it will bring your good to you.

ONE LAW AND MANY MANIFESTATIONS

People often ask if the Law will not bring harm as well as good. This question would never be asked if people understood what Universal Law really means. Of course it will bring us what we think. All law will do the same thing. The law of electricity will either light our house or burn it down. We decide what we are to do with the Law. Law is always impersonal. There is no likelihood of using the Law for harmful purposes if we always use it for the more complete expression of life.

We must not use it for any purpose that we would not like to experience ourselves. This should answer all questions of that nature. Do I really want the thing I ask for? Am I willing to take for myself what I ask for other people? How can we use the Law for evil if we desire only the good? We cannot and we should not bother about it. We want only the good for ourselves and for the whole world; when we have started causation, at once the Law will set to work carrying out our plans. Never distrust the Law and become afraid lest you misuse it. That is a great mistake, all Law is impersonal and cares not who uses it. It will bring to all just what is already in their thought. No person can long use it in a destructive way, for it will destroy him if he persists in doing wrong. We have no responsibility for anyone except ourselves. Get over all idea that you must save the world; we have all tried and have all failed. We may, by demonstrating in our own lives, prove that the Law really exists as the great power behind all things. This is all that we can do.

Everyone must do the same thing for himself. Let the dead bury their dead, and see that you live. In this you are not selfish but are simply proving that law governs your life. All can do the same when they come to believe, and none until they believe.

TRANSCENDING PREVIOUS CONDITIONS

What if at times we attract something that we do not want? What about all the things that we have already attracted into our lives? Must we still suffer until the last farthing be paid? Are we bound by Karma? Yes, in a certain degree we are bound by what we have done; it is impossible to set law in motion and not have it produce. What we sow we must also reap, of that there is no doubt; but here is something to think about; the Bible also says that if a man repents, his "sins are blotted out, and remembered no more forever." Here we have two statements which at first seem not to agree. The first says that we must suffer from what we have done, and the second that under certain conditions we will not have to suffer. What are those conditions? A changed attitude toward the Law. It means that we must stop thinking and acting in the wrong way.

When we do this we are taken out of the old order and established in the new. Someone will say: If that is true, what about the Law of Cause and Effect? Is that broken? No, it is this way: The Law is not broken, it would still work out if we continued to use it in the wrong way; but when we reverse the cause, that is, think and act in a different way, then we have changed the flow of the Law. It is still the same Law but we have changed its flow, so that, instead of limiting us and punishing us, it frees and blesses. It is still the Law but we have changed our attitude toward it. We might throw a ball at the window, and if nothing stopped it, it would break the glass. Here is Law in motion. But if someone catches the ball before it reaches the window, the glass will not be broken. Neither the glass nor the Law will be broken. The flow of Law will be changed, that is all. So can we, no matter what has happened in the past, so transcend the old experience, that it will no longer have any effect upon us. So if we have attracted something that is not best to keep, we will remember that we do not have to keep it. It was the best that we knew at the time, and so was good as far as it went, but now we know more and can do better.

As Law works without variation, so does the Law of attraction work the same way. All that we have to do is to drop the undesired thing from our thought, forgive ourselves and start anew. We must never even think of it again. Let go of it once and for all. Our various experiences will teach us more and more to try to mold all of our thoughts and desires, so that they will be in line with the fundamental purpose of the Great Mind, the expression of that which is perfect. To fear to make conscious use of the Law would be to paralyze all efforts of progress.

More and more will we come to see that a great cosmic plan is being worked out, and that all we have to do is to lend ourselves to it, in order that we may attain unto a real degree of life. As we do subject our thought to the greater purposes we are correspondingly blest, because we are working more in line with the Father, who from the beginning knew the end. We should never lose sight of the fact that we are each given the individual right to use the law, and that we cannot escape from using it.

Let us, then, go forward with the belief that a greater power is working through us; that all law is a law of good; that we have planted our seed of thought in the Mind of the Absolute; and that we can go our way rejoicing in the Divine privilege of working with the Infinite.

UNDERSTANDING AND MISUNDERSTANDING

There are many persons who are constantly unhappy because they seem always to be misunderstood. They find it hard to use the Law of Attraction in an affirmative way, and they keep on drawing to themselves experiences which they would rather have avoided. The trouble with them is that there is always an undercurrent of thought which either neutralizes or destroys whatever helpful thoughts they have set in motion in their moments of greater strength. Such persons are usually very sensitive, and while this is a quality which is most creative when under control, it is most destructive when uncontrolled, because it is most chaotic. They should first come to know the Law and see how it works, and then treat themselves to overcome all sensitiveness. They should realize that everyone in the world is a friend, and prove this by never saying anything unkind to anyone or about anyone. They must within themselves see all people as perfect beings made in the Divine Image; and, seeing nothing else, they will in time be able to say that this is also the way that all people see them. Holding this as the law of their lives they will destroy all negative thought; and then, with that power which is always in a sensitive person, but which is now under control, they will find that life is theirs to do with as they please, the only requirement being that as they sow so must they also reap. We all know that anything that is unlike good is of short duration, but anything that embodies the good is like God, ever present and Eternal. We free ourselves through the same law under which we first bound ourselves.

The ordinary individual unknowingly does something that destroys any possibility of getting good results in the demonstration of prosperity. He affirms his good and makes his unity with it, and this is right, but he does not stop looking at it in others, which is wrong and is the cause of confusion. We cannot affirm a principle and deny it in the same breath. We must become what we want and we will never be able to do that while we still persist in seeing what we do not want, no matter where we see it. We cannot believe that something is possible for us without also believing the same for every individual.

One of the ways of attainment is, of a necessity, the way of universal love: coming to see all as the true sons of God, one with the Infinite Mind. This is no mere sentiment but the clear statement of a fundamental law and that man who does not obey it, is opposing the very thing that brought him into expression. It is true that through mental means alone he may bring to himself things and he may hold them as long as the will lasts. This is the ordinary way, but we want to do more than compel things to appear. What we want is that things should gravitate to us because we are employing the same law that God uses. When we so attain this attitude of mind, then that which is brought into manifestation will never be lost, for it will be as eternal as the law of God and can never be destroyed forever. It is a comfort to know that we do not have to *make* things happen, but that the law of Divine love is all that we will ever need; it will relieve the overworked brain and the fagged muscle just to be still and know that we are One with the ALL in ALL.

How can we enter in, if at one and the same time we are believing for ourselves and beholding the beam in our brother's eye? Does that not obstruct the view and pervert our own natures? We must see only the good and let nothing else enter into our minds. Universal Love of all people and of all things is but returning love to the source of all love, to Him who creates all in love and holds all in divine care. The sun shines on all alike. Shall we separate and divide where God has so carefully united? We are dividing our own things when we do this, and sooner or later the Law of Absolute Justice that weighs out to each one his just measure will balance the account, and then we shall be obliged to suffer for the mistakes we have made. God does not bring this agony on us but we have imposed it on ourselves. If from selfish motives alone, we must love all things and look upon all things as good, made from the substance of the Father.

We can only hope to bring to ourselves that which we draw through the avenue of love. We must watch our thinking and if we have aught against any soul, get rid of it as soon as possible. This is the only safe and sure way. Did not Jesus at the supreme moment of sacrifice ask that the Father forgive all the wrong that was being done to Him? Shall we suppose that we can do it in a better way? If we do not at the present time love all people, then we must learn how to do it, and the way will become easier, when all condemnation is gone forever and we behold only good. God is good and God is Love; more than this we cannot ask nor conceive.

Another thing that we must eliminate is talking about limitation; we must not even think of it or read about it, or have any connection with it in any of our thinking, for we get only that which we think, no more and no less. This will be a hard thing to do. But if we remember that we are working out the science of being, though it may seem long and hard at times we sooner or later do it, and once done it is done forever. Every step in advance is an Eternal step, and will never have to be taken again. We are not building for a day or a year, but we are building for all time and for Eternity. So we will build the more stately mansion under the Supreme wisdom and the unfailing guidance of the Spirit, and we will do unto all, even as we would have them do unto us; there is no other way. The wise will listen, look and learn, then follow what they know to be the only way that is in line with the Divine will and purposes. So shall all see that God is good and in Him is no evil.

NO UNUSUAL EXPERIENCE

In demonstrating the truth of supply we do not have to experience any peculiar emotion or psychic experience. We do not have to feel any thrills or anything of that sort. While it is true that some of these things may come, yet we should remember that what we are doing is dealing with law, and that as law it will obey us, when we comply with its nature and contact it in the right way. What we are doing is stating something into Mind, and if the impression is clear in our own minds *that it is* and *that it is done* we have put all the activity we can put into it, until such a time as something happens in the external for us to work upon. So many people say, "I do wish that I could feel something, when I give a treatment." All this is a mistake and is an attempt to give a physical reason for life. What we do need to feel is that, since God is all and is good, He wants us to have only the good; and feeling this we should take what is already made for us. Our attitude towards such a good Father should constantly be one of thanksgiving. When we begin to prove the power of the truth we will always maintain this attitude. *Know* that you are dealing with a sure thing and that all you have to do is to think positively into it and wait for the results to come in the outer. Then do what your own good sense tells you to do, for this is the thought of God through you. More and more you will find that you are being led out of difficulty into that freedom which is the Divine birthright of every living soul. Go ahead, then, looking only at the things desired and never at the things not wanted. Victory will always be on the side that the majority of your thoughts rest on in absolute acceptance.

VISUALIZING

Some people visualize everything that they think, and many think that it is impossible to make a demonstration unless they possess the power to visualize. This is not the case. While a certain amount of vision is necessary, on the other hand it must be remembered that we are dealing with a power that is like the soil of the ground, which will produce the plant when we plant seed. It does not matter if we have never before seen a plant like the one that is to be made for us. Our thought is the seed and mind is the soil. We are always planting and harvesting. All that we need to do is to plant only that which we want to harvest. This is not difficult to understand. We cannot think poverty and at the same time demonstrate plenty. If a person wants to visualize let him do so, and if he sees himself in full possession of his desire and knows that he is receiving, he will make his demonstration. If, on the other hand, he does not visualize, then let him simply state what he wants and absolutely believe that he has it and the result will always be the same.

Remember that you are always dealing with law and that this is the only way that anything could come into existence. Don't argue over it. That means that you have not as yet become convinced of the truth, or you would not argue. Be convinced and rest in peace.

WHERE DEMONSTRATION TAKES PLACE

Does demonstration take place in the patient, the practitioner or in the mind of God? Let us see; *we are* in the mind of God and so it must take place there. But the patient is also in the mind of God or there would be two minds, and so it must take place in the mind of the patient, also. But that is the mind of God, so what does it matter where it takes place? We do not have to project our thought, because Mind is right at hand and never leaves us at any time. All that we have to do is to know within ourselves, and, when we are absolutely convinced, we will have made the demonstration.

As far as the practitioner is concerned, all that he has to do is to convince himself. Here his work begins and ends. There is a power that will look after the rest. Is this not the supreme attitude of faith in higher power? Of course it is, and the more of that faith that we have, the easier it will be for us and the quicker we will receive an answer to our prayer. If you have a simple, childlike faith it will produce; but it should give us a greater faith when we know something of the way that the law operates. It follows, then, that we should, by under-standing, have so great a faith that we shall never fail to get the affirmative answer to all of our thoughts. Each victory will strengthen us until the time will come when we will no longer have to say *I hope* or *believe*, but *I know*.

PART TWO

Practice

TREATMENTS

The way to give a treatment is first of all to absolutely believe that you can; believe that your word goes forth into a real Creative Power, which at once takes it up, and begins to operate upon it; feel that to this Power all things are possible. It knows nothing but Its own power to do that which It wishes to do. It receives the impress of your thought and acts upon it.

It is never safe to treat for anything that you do not wish to happen. This means that what you would want for another, you must first be willing to receive for yourself.

Believe then that your word is to be acted upon by an Almighty Power; feel its great reality, in and through all things you speak into it; and declare just what you wish it to do for you, never doubting in your own mind but that it will do just as you have directed.

All that a practitioner has to do is to convince himself, to know, to believe, and that thing will happen to him which he states. One of the first things, then, is to be definite; to have a mental likeness of the thing that you desire; to know exactly what you want. This mental likeness, this absolute acceptance of the fact that it now is, must never be overlooked; without it you will not accomplish your desired objective.

We sit down with our own souls, at peace with the world, at peace with ourselves; we realize that we are dealing with something that is a reality, something that cannot fail. We try to get a clear concept of the thing; we rest in that realization, while the Universal Creative Power takes it up and acts upon it.

We have stated just what we wanted done unto us; we have believed; we have believed that we have received; never again will we contradict the fact that we have stated. The person who can do this is sure of getting results.

UNDERSTANDING AND GUIDANCE

The inner man is always in immediate connection with the Infinite of understanding. We are immersed in a living Intelligence; we are surrounded by a Power that knows, for "in Him we live and move and have our being."

If our outer thought were never confused, we should at all times draw from this Infinite source of knowledge; we should be guided by It and never make mistakes; our minds would be like the smooth surface of a lake, unruffled by wind and storm.

But with most of us this is not the case; we become confused in the outer so that the surface of the mind is in turmoil, no longer clear and transparent, and we cannot get the clear vision, the real guidance, and we get things wrong because we do not see clearly.

The development of the understanding is learning to draw from the Infinite understanding; we can never do this while we are confused in our thinking.

The first thing to do when we wish a greater understanding is to be still and listen to the inner voice, to withdraw for a few moments into the silence of the soul taking here what we already know, and realizing that a greater intelligence is enlarging it.

Here we indefinitely take the pattern of our thought, the thing that we are working on, and ask for, and receive, new light; we hold this up in Divine Light and try to believe that we are being guided; we state that Supreme Intelligence and Absolute Power are acting upon our thought and bringing it to pass; it is now guiding us and we shall make no mistake; we hold ourselves in the secret place of the Most High, and abide under the shadow of the Almighty.

HOW TO KNOW JUST WHAT TO DO

Often we find ourselves confronted by the problem of how to begin. We are not sure *what* we want to do; we see no *way* to begin anything; see nothing to begin on; when we find ourselves in this position, humanly speaking, not knowing where to turn, then of all times we must be quiet and listen; then of all times we must trust that the same power that *started all things* will also *start us* in the right road, for without some superior power we shall surely fail.

How often do people in the business world find themselves in this position? They realize that something must be done, but what? How can they get the right idea?

Here we must wait and know that the same Power that first thought a universe into being can also think our world and work into being. It knows all things; It knows how to begin and It cannot fail; we wish in some way to connect with this Power that will never fail us, so we may draw from it some idea with which to begin.

We must realize that there is something that wants to respond, to make manifest and in this realization wait for the idea; it may not come at first, but we must be patient, never doubting, and waiting thus in faith, it *will* come.

I once knew a businessman who was connected with a firm that had always been very successful, but at that time something had occurred that was causing them to lose out. This had gone on for a year and things were going from bad to worse. Failure seemed inevitable. He became interested in New Thought. He was told he could draw an idea from the Infinite and work it out on the plane of the visible. He told his partners that he wished to go home for a few days and that when he came back he would have worked out an idea which would put the business on a successful basis. They laughed at him, as people generally laugh at something they do not understand, but having no other plan they gave their consent. He went home and for three days sat in deep thought, claiming Supreme guidance and absolute leading of the Spirit. During this time a complete plan formulated in his mind as to the exact method to pursue in the business. He returned and told his plan to his partners. Again they laughed, saying it could not be done in business; could not be done any way; it would not work. But again they consented, knowing it was this or failure.

He then went to work carrying out all the details of his thought, following each leading that had come to him during those three days, and within a year he brought the failing business to a standard that transcended anything they had ever before experienced. He proved the law and became such an expert, that he gave up his business and devoted his entire time to helping other people do the same for themselves as he had done.

What this man did anyone can do if he will follow the same course and refuse to become discouraged. There is a Power that simply awaits our recognition of It, to spring into our thought as an unfailing leading, an unerring guidance. To those who lean on the ever outstretched arm of the Infinite, life is big with limitless possibilities.

We must wait and listen, then go about our outer business with an inner conviction that we are being led into a more perfect expression of life. All can do this.

FOLLOWING UP A THOUGHT

When we feel that we do have the right leading, when that something inside us tells us that we are led, then no matter what it appears like, we must follow it up. Something beyond our intelligence is doing the thing through us and we must do nothing to contradict it.

Perhaps it will cause us to do something that seems to go contrary to the experience of the race. This makes no difference. All advance in invention and all advance along any line has always gone ahead of what the experience of the race thinks is possible.

Great men are the ones who get a vision and then go to work to make it come true, never looking to one side but with one-pointedness and calm determination, stick to the thing until it is accomplished.

It may take much patience and a great deal of faith, but the end is as sure as is the reality of a Supreme Being itself.

Never hesitate to trust in that inner leading, never fear but it will be right. We are all in the midst of Supreme Intelligence; It presses against the doors of our thought, waiting to be known. We must be open to It at all times, ready to receive direction and to be guided into greater truths.

THE SINGLE STREAM
OF THOUGHT

We are all in Mind, and what we think into it is taken up and done unto us. This means that *as* we think it will be done. We cannot think one way one day and change our thought the next and hope to get the desired results. We must be very clear in our thought, sending out only such thoughts as we wish to see manifested in our condition.

Here is something worth remembering. Unless we are working with people who think as we do, we had better be working alone. One stream of thought, even though it may not be very powerful, will do more for us than many powerful streams that are at variance with each other. This means that, unless we are sure that we are working with people who harmonize, we would better work alone. Of course we cannot retire from business simply because people do not agree with us, but what we can do is to keep our thoughts to ourselves. We do not have to leave the world in order to control our thought; but we do have to learn that we can stay right in the world and still think just what we want to think, regardless of what others are thinking.

One single stream of thought, daily sent out into Creative Mind, will do wonders. Within a year the person who will practice this will have completely changed his conditions of life.

The way to practice this is daily to spend some time in thinking and in mentally seeing just what is wanted; see the thing just as it is wished and then affirm that this is now done. Try to feel that what has been stated is the truth.

Words and affirmations simply give shape to thought; they are not creative. Feeling is creative and the more feeling that is put into the word the greater power it will have over conditions. In doing this we think of the condition only as an effect, something that follows what we think. It cannot help following our thought. This is the way that all creation comes into expression.

It is a great help to realize mentally that at all times a great stream of thought and power is operating through us; it is constantly going out into Mind, where it is taken up and acted upon. Our business is to keep that stream of thought just where we want it to be: to be ready at any time to act when the impulse comes for action. Our action must never be negative, it must always be affirmative, for we are dealing with something that cannot fail. We may fail to realize, but the Power in itself is Infinite and cannot fail.

We are setting in motion in the Absolute a stream of thought that will never cease until it accomplishes its purpose. Try to feel this, be filled with a great joy as you feel that it is given to you to use this great and only Power.

Keep the thought clear and never worry about the way that things seem to be going. Let go of all outer conditions when working in Mind, for there is where things are made; there creation is going on, and It is now making something for us. This must be believed as never believed before; It must be known as the great reality; It must be felt as the only Presence. There is no other way to obtain.

Though all the Infinite may want to give, yet we must take, and, as far as we are concerned, that taking is mental. Though people may laugh at this, even that does not matter. "He laughs best who laughs last." We know in "what we believe," and that will be sufficient.

ENLARGING OUR THOUGHT

We can never stand still in our thought. Either we will be growing or else we will be going back. As we can attract to ourselves only that of which we first have a mental likeness, it follows that if we wish to attract larger things we must provide larger thoughts. This enlarging of consciousness is so necessary that too much cannot be said about it.

Most people get only a short way and then stop: they cannot seem to get beyond a certain point; they can do so much and no more. Why is it that a person in business does just about so much each year? We see people in all walks of life, getting so far, never going beyond a certain point. There must be a reason for everything; nothing happens, if all is governed by law, and we can come to no other conclusion.

When we look into the mental reason for things we find out why things happen. The man who gets so far and never seems to go beyond that point is still governed by law; when he allows his thoughts to take him out into larger fields of action, his conditions come up to his thought; when he stops enlarging his thought he stops growing. If he would still keep on in thought, realizing more and still more, he would find that in the outer form of things he would be doing greater things.

There are many reasons why a man stops thinking larger things. One of them is a lack of imagination. He cannot conceive of anything more to follow than that which has already happened. Another thought works like this: "This is as far as anyone can go in my business." Right here he signs his own death warrant. Often a person will say, "I am too old to do bigger things." There he stops. Someone else will say, "Competition is too great"; and here is where this man stops; he can go no further than his thought will carry him.

All this is unnecessary when we realize that life is first of all Consciousness, and then conditions follow. We see no reason why a man should not go on and on, and never stop growing. No matter what age or what circumstance, if life is thought, we can keep on thinking bigger things. There is no reason why a man who is already doing well should not be able mentally to conceive of a still better condition. What if we are active? There is always a greater activity possible. We can still see a little beyond what has come before. This is just what we should do, see, even though it be but a little beyond our former thought. If we always practice this, we will find that every year we shall be growing, every month we shall be advancing; and as time goes on we shall become really great. As there is no stopping in that Power which is Infinite, as the Limitless is without bounds, so should we keep on trying to see more and greater possibilities in life.

We should definitely work every day for the expansion of thought. If we have fifty customers a day we should endeavor to believe that we have sixty. When we have sixty we should mentally see seventy. This should never stop; there is no stopping place in Mind.

Let go of everything else, drop everything else from your thought, and mentally see more coming to you than has ever come before; believe that Mind is establishing this unto you, and then go about your business in the regular way. Never see the limitation; never dwell upon it, and above all things else never talk limitation to anyone; this is the only way, and there is no other way to grow a larger thought. The man with the big thought is always the man who does big things in life. Get hold of the biggest thing that you can think of and claim it for your own; mentally see it and hold it as a thing already done, and you will prove to yourself that life is without bounds.

ALWAYS BE GATHERING

There is no reason why a person should ever stop. This does not mean that we should be miserly, trying to accumulate more and more to hold, but that our thought should so enlarge that it cannot help gathering more and more, even though, on the other hand, or with the other hand, we are ever distributing that which we gather. Indeed, the only reason for having is that we may give out of that which we have.

No matter what big thing happens to us we should still be expecting more and more. Even when we think that we have at last arrived; right at the moment when it seems as though life had given us all that we could stand; right here let it be but a beginning for still greater things.

No matter how large the picture that you hold in mind, make it larger. The reason why so many people come to the point where they stop is that they come to a point where they stop growing in their own minds. They come to a point where they can see no more, thinking that because they have really done a big thing they should stop there. We must watch our thought for signs of inactivity. Nothing in the universe ever stops. Everything is built on a boundless basis, drawn from a limitless source, come forth from an Infinite sea of unmanifest life. We speak forth into this life and draw back from it all that we first think into it. Life is always limitless, and the only thing that limits us is our inability to conceive mentally, and we should draw more and more from that limitless source.

MENTAL LIKENESS

We can draw from the Infinite only as much as we first think into it. It is at this point that so many fail, thinking that all they need to do is to affirm what they want and it will follow. While it *is* true that affirmations have real power, it is also true that they have *only* that which we speak into them.

As we cannot speak a word that we do not know, so we cannot make an affirmation that we do not understand. We really affirm only that which we know to be true; we know that to be true which we have experienced within ourselves. Although we may have heard or read that this or that thing is true, it is only when there is something within our own souls that corresponds or recognizes its truth, that it is true to us. This ought never to be lost sight of: we can effectively affirm only that which we know, and we know only that which we are. It is herein that we see the necessity of providing within a greater concept of life, a bigger idea of ourselves and a more expanded concept of the Universe in which we live, move and have our being. This is a matter of inner growth together with the enlarging of all lines of thought and activity.

If we want to do a thing that is really worth doing, we must mentally grow until we are that thing, which we want to see made flesh. This may take time, but we should be glad to use all the time necessary to our own development.

But few people in limitation have a mental likeness of plenty. This likeness must be provided. The thought must be large enough to cover the whole of the thing desired; a small thought will produce only a small thing. The very fact that all is Mind proves this to be true. All *is* Mind and, because it is, we can draw from that Mind only that which we first think into it as a reality. We must become the thing we want. We must see it, think it, realize it, before the creative power of Mind can work it out for us. This is an inner process of the expansion of consciousness. It is a thought, growing and realizing within. All can do this who wish and who will take the time and trouble, but it will mean work. The majority of people are too lazy to make the effort.

Daily we must train our thought to see that only which we wish to experience, and since we are growing into what we are mentally dwelling upon, we should put all small and insignificant thoughts and ideals out of our thinking and see things in a larger way. We must cultivate the habit of an enlarged mental horizon, daily seeing farther and farther ahead, and so experiencing larger and greater things in our daily life.

A good practice for the enlargement of thought is daily to see ourselves in a little bigger place, filled with more of activity, surrounded with increased influence and power; feel more and more that things are coming to us; see that much more is just ahead, and so far as possible, know that we now have all that we see and all that we feel. Affirm that you are that larger thing; that you are now entered into that larger life; feel that something within is drawing more to you; live with the idea and let the concept grow, expecting only the biggest and the best to happen. Never let small thoughts come into your mind, and you will soon find that a larger and greater experience has come into your life.

KEEPING THE THING
IN MIND

Never let go of the mental image until it becomes manifested. Daily bring up the clear picture of what is wanted and impress it on the mind as an accomplished fact. This impressing on our own minds the thought of what we wish to realize will cause our own minds to impress the same thought on Universal Mind. In this way we shall be praying without ceasing. We do not have to hold continually the thought of something we want in order to get it, but the thought that we may inwardly become the thing we want. Fifteen minutes, twice each day, is time enough to spend in order to demonstrate anything, but the rest of the time ought also to be spent constructively. That is, we must stop all negative thinking and give over all wrong thought, holding fast to the realization that it is now done unto us. We must know that we are dealing with the only power there is in the Universe; that there is none other beside it, and that we are in it partaking of its nature and its laws. Always, behind the word that we send forth, must be the calm confidence in our ability to speak into the power, and the willingness of Mind to execute for us. We must gradually grow in confidence and in trust in the unseen world of spiritual activity. This is not hard, if we but remember that the Spirit makes things out of Itself by simply becoming the thing that it makes, and since there is no other power to oppose it, it will always work. The Spirit will never fail us if we never fail to believe in its goodness and its responsiveness.

Life will become one grand song, when we realize that since God is for us, none can be against us. We shall cease merely to exist; we shall *live*.

DESTROY ALL THOUGHTS THAT WE DO NOT WISH TO EXPERIENCE

We must resolutely set our faces to the rising consciousness of the Son of Truth; seeing only the One Power we must destroy the adversary and leave the field to God or Good. All that is in any way negative must be wiped off the slate and we must daily come into the higher thought, to be washed clean of the dust and chaos of the objective life. In the silence of the soul's communion with the Great Cause of All Being, into the stillness of the Absolute, into the secret place of the Most High, back of the din and the ceaseless roar of life, we shall find a resting place and a place of real spiritual power. Speak in this inner silence and say, "I am one with the Almighty; I am one with all life, with all power, with all presence. I AM, I AM, I AM." Listen to the silence. From out of the seeming void the voice of peace will answer the waiting soul, "All is well."

Here we make known all our needs and wants, and here we receive first hand from the Infinite all that we shall ever need to make life healthy, happy and harmonious. Few enter here, because of the belief that conditions and circumstances control. Know that there is no law but God's law; that the soul sets its own law in the Infinite and that our slightest wish is honored by the Father Mind.

Daily practice the truth and daily die to all error-thought. Spend more time receiving and realizing the presence of the Most High and less time worrying. Wonderful power will come to the one who believes and trusts in that Power in which he has come to believe. Know that all good and all God is with you; All Life and All Power; and never again say, "I fear," but always, "I trust, because 'I know in whom I have believed.'"

DIRECT PRACTICE FOR PROSPERITY

S uppose that you are doing a mail-order business and sending out cards to the whole country. Take the cards into your hands, or simply think of them and declare into the only Mind that they will accomplish that for which they are sent out; know that every word written on them is truth and carries its own conviction with it; see them each reaching that place where it will be received with gladness and read with interest; declare this to be so *now*; feel it to be the truth; mentally assert that each card will find its way to the exact place where it will be wanted and where it will benefit the receiver; feel that each card is cared for by the Spirit; that it is a messenger of truth and power and that it will carry conviction and realization with it. When the word is spoken always feel that Mind at once takes it up and never fails to act upon it. Our place in the creative order is to know this and to be willing to do all that we can without hurry or worry, and, above all else, to trust absolutely in the Spirit to do the rest. He who sees most clearly and believes most implicitly will make the greatest demonstration. This one should be *you*, and will be you as soon as the false thought is gone and the realization that there is but the one Power and the one Presence comes. We are wrapped in an Infinite Love and Intelligence and we should cover ourselves with it and claim its protection from all evil. Declare that your word is the presence and the activity of the Power of all that is and wait for the perfect concept to unfold.

RACE CONSCIOUSNESS

One of the things which greatly hinders us from demonstrating a greater degree of prosperity we may call race thought or race consciousness. This is the result of all that the race has thought or believed. We are immersed in it, and those who are receptive to it are controlled by it. All thought seeks expression along the lines of least resistance. When we become negative or fearful we attract that kind of thought and condition. We must be sure of ourselves; we must be positive; we must not be aggressive, but absolutely sure and poised within. Negative people are always picking up negative conditions; they get into trouble easily. Persons who are positive draw positive things; they are always successful. Few people realize that the law of thought is the great reality; that thoughts produce things. When we come to understand this power of thought, we will carefully watch our thinking to see that no thought enters that we do not want made into a *thing*.

We can guard our minds by knowing that no negative thought can enter; we can daily practice by saying that no race thought of limitation can enter the mind; that Spirit forms itself around us and protects us from all fear and from all limitation. Let us clothe ourselves in the great realization that all power is ours and that nothing else can enter; let us fill the atmosphere of our homes, and places of business with streams of positive thought. Other people will feel this and will like to be near us and enter into the things that we enter into. In this way we shall be continually drawing only the best.

DEVELOPING INTUITION

If a person always lived near to Mind he would never make any great mistakes. Some seem to have the faculty of always knowing just what is best to do; they always succeed because they avoid making errors. We can all so train ourselves that we will be guided by the Supreme Mind of the Universe; but we can never do this until we believe that we can receive direct from the source of all knowledge. This is done by sitting in the silence and knowing that the Spirit is inwardly directing us. We should try to feel that our thought is being permeated by the thought of the Spirit. We should expect It to direct but should never become discouraged if at once a direct impression is not received. The work is going on even if it is not seen or even felt. Thought is forming in our mind and in time will come forth as an idea. When the idea does come always trust in it even though it may not seem to be quite as we had expected. The first impressions are usually the most direct and the clearest; they are generally direct from the Mind of the Universe and should be carefully worked out into expression.

We declare as we sit in the silence that the Spirit of all knowledge is making known within us just what we should do; that it is telling us just what to say or where to go. Have absolute reliance on this as it is one of the most important things to do. We should always get that inner assurance before undertaking any new enterprise; being sure that we have really put the whole thing into the hands of life and that all that we have to do is to work it out in the outer. We shall learn to avoid mistakes when we learn to be directed by that inner voice that never makes mistakes. We should declare in the silence that Intelligence is guiding us and it will do so.

PRESENCE OF ACTIVITY

Suppose that your place of business does not seem to manifest any activity; that is, suppose that customers do not come. To the person in the business world the presence of customers generally means activity. Suppose that you have come to believe that the principle will work in the smallest as well as in the greatest things. What you want now is a greater activity. How are you going to see activity when there is none?

Here is a great question in Truth. Must we overlook that which we see, and that which we have experienced? Yes, absolutely; there is no other way. If we keep on seeing the thing as it appears we will never be able to change its appearance. What we must do, then, in spite of the seeming inactivity, is still to know and mentally to see and declare that we are in the midst of activity. Feel this to be true; mentally see the place crowded; know that it is packed full of customers all the time; declare that your word draws them in; have no sense of strain about it whatever; simply know that you are dealing with the only Power that there is; it will work; it must work. Realize when you have spoken the word that a greater Power has taken it up and that it is being established unto you. Have no idea of limitation; speak forth into Mind with perfect trust. If you have the ability mentally to see the place full, combine this with the word, and daily visualize it as being filled. Always combine faith in the Higher Power with all that you do; feel that you are being especially looked after. This is true. When a soul turns to the Universe of unmanifest life, at the same time It turns toward him. Jesus told this in the story of the Prodigal Son; the Father saw him afar off. Always there is that inward turning to us of the Parent Mind when we turn to It and place ourselves in closer contact with Life.

We must keep our mind clear so that when the Spirit brings the gift we will be open to receive it. Even God cannot force things upon us. We must receive even before we see.

For the feeble hands and helpless,
Groping blindly in the darkness
Touch God's right hand in that darkness
And are lifted up and strengthened.

Always, when we believe, we will have that belief honored to the Spirit of Life. Mentally seeing just what we want; still seeing even though the heavens fall, we shall succeed in proving that the law of life is a law of liberty. God made man to have all that the Universe contained and then left him alone to discover his own nature.

Stop all striving and all struggle and within your own soul know the Truth and trust absolutely in it. Daily declare that you are being guided and protected and that the power of the Spirit is bringing all to pass, and wait in perfect peace and confidence. Such an attitude of mind will overcome anything and will prove that spiritual thought force is the only real power in the Universe.

DRAWING YOUR OWN TO YOU

Suppose that you wish to draw friends and companions to you; that you wish to enlarge your circle of friendships. This, too, can all be worked out by law, for everything can be worked out by the same law, the reason being that all is One and that the One becomes the many in expression. There are too many people in the world who are lonesome because they have a sense of separation from people. The thing to do is not to try to unify *with* people, but *with the Principle of Life* behind all people and things. This is working from the center and not the circumference; in this One Mind are the minds of all people. When you unite your thought with the whole you will be united with the parts of the whole. The first thing to do, then, is to realize that Life is your friend and companion; feel the divine companionship; feel that you are one with all life; declare that, as this thought awakens within your mind, so does it awaken within the mind of the whole race; feel that the world is being drawn to you; love the world and everyone who is in it; include all, if you would be included *in* all. The world seeks strength; be strong. The world loves love; embody it; see the good in all people; let go of all else. People will feel your love and will be drawn into it. Love is the greatest power in the Universe; it is at the base of all else; it is the cause of all that is. Feel your love to be like a great light lighting the pathway of the whole world; it will come back to you bringing so many friends that there will not be time enough to enjoy them all. Become a real friend and you will have many friends.

Be sufficient unto yourself and at the same time include all else, and people will feel your strength and will have a desire to come into the radiance of it. Never become unhappy or morbid; always be cheerful and radiate good nature and happiness; never look depressed or down in the mouth; the world is attracted to the strongest center of cheer and good fellowship. Never allow your feelings to be hurt. No one wants to hurt you, and none could, even though they did want to; you are above all that. Wherever you go know that the Spirit of Truth goes before and prepares the way, bringing to you every friend and influence that will be necessary to your comfort and well being. This is not selfishness but good sense and will surely bring to you a harvest of friends and companions.

Declare unto Mind that you are now linked with all

people and that all people are linked with you: see yourself surrounded with hosts of friends; mentally feel their presence and rejoice that all good is yours now. Do this no matter what seems to happen, and it will not be long before you will meet wonderful friends and will be brought into touch with the great of the world.

THE FINAL WORD

In the last analysis, man is just what he thinks himself to be; he is big in capacity if he thinks big thoughts; he is small if he thinks small thoughts. He will attract to himself what he thinks most about. He can learn to govern his own destiny when he learns to control his thoughts. In order to do this he must first realize that everything in the manifest universe is the result of some inner activity of Mind. This Mind is God, producing a universe by the activity of His own divine thoughts; man is in this Mind as a thinking center, and what he thinks governs his life, even as God's thought governs the Universe, by setting in motion all the cosmic activities. This is so easy to understand, and so plain as to use that we often wonder why we have been so long finding out this, the greatest of all truths of all the ages. Believing; thinking what is believed to be true; thinking into Mind each day that which is wished to be returned; eliminating negative thoughts; thinking positive thoughts; giving thanks to the Spirit of Life that it is so trusting always in the higher Law; never arguing with one's self or with others; using; these are the steps which, when followed, will bring us to where we shall not have to ask if it be true, for, having demonstrated, *we shall know.*

The seed that falls into the ground shall bear fruit of its own kind; and nothing shall hinder it.

"He that hath ears to hear, let him hear."

About the Author

Ernest Holmes (1887–1960) was an internationally recognized authority on religious psychology and the founder of the Religious Science movement. There are currently hundreds of churches and spiritual centers across the country that are based on his teaching, and three international organizations dedicated to his philosophy: United Church of Religious Science, Religious Science International, and Associated New Thought Network. Holmes's writings and philosophy have influenced countless teachers and authors, and have inspired millions. His beloved books include the seminal text *The Science of Mind, This Thing Called You, Creative Mind, Creative Mind and Success, The Art of Life* (previously published as *This Thing Called Life*), *Love and Law, Prayer, The Hidden Power of the Bible, The Essential Ernest Holmes,* and *365 Science of Mind.*

You can find more information about Holmes and his teachings at www.scienceofmind.com.

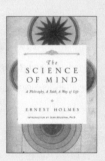

"There is a power for good in this Universe greater than you, and you can use it."

—ERNEST HOLMES

A Treasury of Inspiration and Guidance

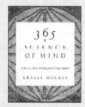

365 Science of Mind

978-1-58542-609-6

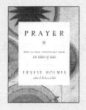

Prayer

978-1-58542-605-8

The Hidden Power
of the Bible

978-1-58542-511-2

Love and Law:
The Unpublished
Teachings

978-1-58542-302-6

The Essential
Ernest Holmes

978-1-58542-181-7

TARCHER
PENGUIN

www.penguin.com

www.scienceofmind.com